The Nacho Manifesto

Jack
Campbell

The
Nacho
Manifesto

Smith
Street
Books

CONTENTS

Manifesto *(noun)*
– A public declaration of policy and aims.

The Nacho Manifesto *(noun)*
– There are many snack foods, but the one true, great
and good snack food is the almighty *nacho*. Our explicit
aim is to persuade and educate the nacho non-believers
through 40 unbelievably delicious, crunchy, diverse and
cheese-laden recipes. We know we'll have your vote.

BASICS

CLASSIC TORTILLA CHIPS

SERVES 4

Pour some oil into a deep-fryer or large deep saucepan, to no more than one-third full. Heat the oil to 180°C (350°F) on a thermometer.

Deep-fry the tortillas in batches, stirring occasionally with a slotted spoon, for 2–3 minutes, or until golden and crisp, bringing the oil back to temperature between each batch. Remove with a slotted spoon, drain on paper towel and season with salt.

Alternatively, the tortilla chips can be baked, rather than fried. Preheat the oven to 160°C (320°F) fan-forced. Spread the tortilla pieces over several baking trays in a single layer. Bake for 8–10 minutes, or until lightly coloured; the tortilla chips will crisp on cooling.

The tortilla chips can be stored in an airtight container for up to 2 days, and refreshed in a 160°C (320°F) fan-forced oven for 5 minutes if necessary.

NOTE

Homemade tortilla chips are particularly good for saucy or wetter toppings — they retain their crunch and texture for longer, won't disintegrate if they become soaked with moisture, and their texture becomes pleasingly chewy.

The cooking time will vary depending on the type of tortilla used, so a bit of experimentation with timing may be necessary.

- Traditional corn tortillas tend to be slightly thicker and drier than mass-produced tortillas.

- Long-life tortillas are slightly higher in moisture and sugar content, so they may take a little longer to cook — but will then over-cook quickly.

- Stale tortillas are great for tortilla chips; they will take a little less time to cook.

vegetable oil,
for deep-frying

300 g (10½ oz) good-quality
corn tortillas (about 15),
torn or cut into quarters

GUACAMOLE

MAKES ABOUT 1½ CUPS

Crush the onion, chilli and chopped coriander stalks with a pinch of salt using a mortar and pestle, or with a fork on a chopping board.

Cut the avocados in half, discarding the stones. Scoop out the flesh and place in a bowl. Add the onion mixture, lime juice and a generous pinch of salt and freshly ground black pepper. Roughly mash the mixture together with a whisk or fork. (Using a whisk may sound a bit strange, but it works really well: it's super quick and roughly chops up the avocado, leaving a good amount of texture.)

Fold in the chopped coriander leaves. Season to taste with a little more salt, pepper and/or lime juice.

Serve immediately, or press a double layer of plastic wrap over the surface of the guacamole and refrigerate until required. It will keep in the refrigerator for up to 2 days.

VARIATIONS

Tomato guacamole: Add a finely chopped tomato to the mixture.

Roasted garlic guacamole: Preheat the oven to 180°C (350°F) fan-forced. Remove any loose papery skin from the outside of 1 whole garlic bulb, then trim off the top 5 mm (¼ inch) of the bulb, leaving the bulb intact. Place it on a square of foil, cut side up, drizzle 1 tablespoon olive oil over the cut surfaces and sprinkle with a little salt. Wrap the foil around the garlic and place directly on an oven rack. Roast for 35–40 minutes, or until soft. Remove from the oven and set aside to cool. Squeeze out the roasted garlic flesh and stir it through the onion mixture.

Tomatillo guacamole: Add 3 chopped roasted (or tinned) tomatillos to the mixture.

Chipotle guacamole: Stir in 1 chopped chipotle chilli in adobo sauce, along with a teaspoon or two of the adobo sauce.

sea salt, to taste

large handful
of coriander (cilantro),
including the stalks and
leaves, chopped separately

2 ripe avocados

¼ small white
onion, finely
chopped

juice of ½ lime,
plus extra, to taste

½ fresh jalapeño
chilli, seeded and
finely chopped

13

REFRIED BEANS (FRIJOLES REFRITOS)

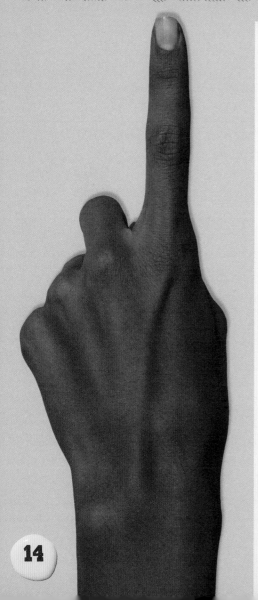

MAKES ABOUT 1½ CUPS

Heat the lard or oil in a heavy-based frying pan over medium—low heat and cook the onion and garlic, stirring occasionally, for 5—6 minutes, or until tender. Add the spices and cook, stirring, for 1 minute.

Add the beans and stock or water to the pan. Mash the beans with a masher or wooden spoon, to a coarse purée. Cook for a further 6—8 minutes, or until the beans have thickened and start to dry out around the side of the pan; add a little more stock or water if the mixture is very thick. Season to taste with salt and freshly ground black pepper.

Serve immediately, or store in an airtight container in the refrigerator for up to 3 days.

Reheat before serving, adding a little stock or water to thin the mixture down if necessary.

2 garlic cloves, crushed

400 g (14 oz) tin beans, such as pinto, borlotti (cranberry), black or red kidney beans, drained

125 ml (4 fl oz/½ cup) chicken stock or water, approximately

1 onion, chopped

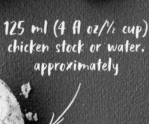

¼–½ teaspoon chilli powder, to taste

1 teaspoon ground cumin

1 tablespoon lard or olive oil

ROASTED
TOMATO SALSA

MAKES ABOUT 2 CUPS

Preheat the oven to 180°C (350°F) fan-forced.

Put the tomatoes in a roasting tin and roast for 25–30 minutes, or until the skin is wrinkled, the tomatoes are starting to collapse, and are charred in spots. Remove from the oven and set aside to cool slightly. Peel away and discard the skin.

Blend or process the onion, garlic and chilli until almost puréed. Add the tomatoes and blend until just combined. Season to taste with salt and freshly ground black pepper.

Serve warm or cold. The salsa will keep in an airtight container in the refrigerator for up to 4 days.

VARIATIONS

Roasted onion & tomato salsa:
Add a quartered whole onion to the roasting tin with the tomatoes.

Roasted capsicum & tomato salsa:
Add a quartered red capsicum (bell pepper) to the roasting tin with the tomatoes, after removing the seeds and membranes.

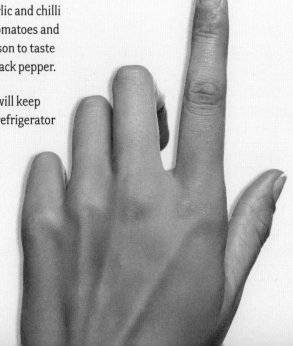

½ fresh jalapeño chilli; for a milder salsa, remove the seeds and membranes

6 roma (plum) tomatoes, cored

1 small garlic clove, peeled

¼ white onion, roughly chopped

sea salt, to taste

17

CHIPOTLE MAYO

MAKES ABOUT 1 CUP

Whisk the mustard, egg yolk and lime juice together in a bowl. Whisking constantly, add the oil in a very slow trickle, until all the oil is incorporated and the mayonnaise is thick and emulsified. Do not add the oil too quickly, or the mayonnaise may separate.

Whisk in the chilli and adobo sauce, or the chilli powder, and season to taste with sea salt. If the mayonnaise is very thick, you can thin it with a little warm water.

Store in an airtight container, with the surface covered closely with plastic wrap, in the refrigerator for up to 3 days.

VARIATION

Garlic aïoli: Add 1 crushed garlic clove to the mustard, egg yolk and lime juice, and omit the chipotle chilli and adobo sauce.

sea salt,
to taste

½ chipotle chilli in 1 teaspoon
adobo sauce, finely chopped, or
1 teaspoon chipotle chilli powder

250 ml (8½ fl oz/
1 cup) mild olive oil
or canola oil

1 egg yolk,
at room
temperature

1 teaspoon
dijon mustard

1 tablespoon
lime juice

19

PICO DE GALLO

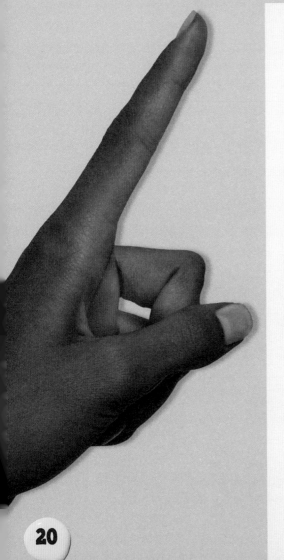

MAKES ABOUT 1½ CUPS

Toss the tomatoes and salt together in a colander or strainer, set over a bowl. Allow to drain for 20–30 minutes, then discard the liquid.

Combine the drained tomatoes with the onion, chilli, coriander and lime juice. Toss to combine and season to taste with salt.

The pico de gallo can be stored for up to 3 days in a sealed container in the refrigerator.

NOTE

You can prepare this recipe without salting the tomato. The flavour won't be quite as intense, but it will still taste good!

3 large ripe tomatoes, finely chopped

1 tablespoon lime juice

1-2 fresh serrano or jalapeño chillies, finely chopped; for a milder salsa, remove the seeds and membranes

½ white onion, finely chopped

½ teaspoon salt, plus extra to taste

25 g (1 oz/½ cup) finely chopped coriander (cilantro) leaves

21

CLASSICS

QUICK CHIPOTLE BEEF NACHOS

SERVES 4–6

1 tablespoon vegetable oil

1 onion, chopped

3 tablespoons tomato paste (concentrated purée)

2 teaspoons ground cumin

2 garlic cloves, crushed

500 g (1 lb 2 oz) minced (ground) beef

300 g (10½ oz) tin kidney beans, drained

250 ml (8½ fl oz/1 cup) beer

2 chipotle chillies in adobo sauce, chopped, plus 2 teaspoons of the adobo sauce

large handful of coriander (cilantro), including the stalks and leaves, chopped, plus extra to serve

1 quantity Classic tortilla chips (page 10), or 250 g (9 oz) store-bought tortilla chips

250 g (9 oz/2 cups) grated mature cheddar

shredded lettuce, to serve

200 g (7 oz) cherry tomatoes, halved

1 avocado, chopped

sour cream or Chipotle mayo (page 18), to serve

sliced pickled jalapeño chillies, to serve

Heat the oil in a frying pan over medium–low heat and cook the onion, stirring often, for 5–6 minutes, or until softened. Add the tomato paste, cumin and garlic and cook, stirring, for 2 minutes.

Increase the heat to medium–high and add the beef. Cook, stirring, for 6–8 minutes, or until the beef changes colour. Stir in the kidney beans, beer, chopped chipotle chillies, adobo sauce and chopped coriander stalks. Bring to the boil, then reduce the heat and simmer, uncovered, for about 15 minutes, or until the liquid is almost evaporated and the mixture has thickened. Stir in the coriander leaves and season to taste with salt and freshly ground black pepper.

Preheat the oven to 170°C (340°F) fan-forced. Spread half the tortilla chips over the base of a baking tray or baking dish suitable for serving. Scatter with half the cheese, and top with a little less than half the beef mixture.

Repeat with a second layer of tortilla chips, most of the cheese (reserve some for the top), the remaining beef and then the remaining cheese.

Bake for 5 minutes, or until the tortilla chips are lightly toasted and the cheese is melted.

Top with the lettuce, tomato, avocado, sour cream and jalapeño chilli. Serve immediately.

QUICK
CHIPOTLE
BEEF NACHOS

BAJA FISH NACHOS

SERVES 4

1 quantity Pickled cabbage slaw (page 48)

400 g (14 oz) firm white fish fillet, such as blue-eye trevalla

1 teaspoon ground cumin

½ teaspoon chilli powder

25 ml (1 fl oz) lime juice

olive oil spray, for cooking

1 quantity Classic tortilla chips (page 10), or 250 g (9 oz) store-bought tortilla chips

100 g (3½ oz) queso fresco or Danish feta, crumbled

coriander (cilantro) leaves, to serve

hot sauce, to serve

BAJA SAUCE

250 g (9 oz/1 cup) plain Greek-style yoghurt

2 handfuls of coriander (cilantro), chopped

4 teaspoons lime juice

½ teaspoon mild chilli powder, or to taste

Make the pickled cabbage slaw, if you don't already have some in the refrigerator.

Sprinkle the fish all over with the cumin and chilli powder. Place in a glass or ceramic bowl and add the lime juice. Set aside to marinate for 10 minutes.

Combine all the baja sauce ingredients in a small bowl. Season to taste with salt and freshly ground black pepper, mixing well. Cover and refrigerate until required.

Heat a barbecue or heavy-based frying pan over medium–high heat. Remove the fish from the lime juice, shaking off the excess liquid, and spray the fish with olive oil. Cook for 3–4 minutes on each side, or until browned and cooked through; the cooking time will depend on the thickness of the fillet. Gently flake the fish into large chunks.

Meanwhile, preheat the oven to 170°C (340°F) fan-forced. Spread the tortilla chips over the base of a baking tray or baking dish suitable for serving. Bake for 5 minutes, or until the tortilla chips are lightly toasted.

Drizzle the warm tortilla chips with about half the baha sauce. Top with the fish, spoonfuls of the slaw and the remaining sauce. Scatter with the cheese and coriander, and splash with hot sauce. Serve immediately.

BAJA FISH NACHOS

MEATBALL NACHOS WITH CHEESE SAUCE

SERVES 4

1 quantity Classic tortilla chips (page 10), or 250 g (9 oz) store-bought tortilla chips

1 quantity Pico de gallo (page 20)

sliced pickled jalapeño chillies, to serve

coriander (cilantro), to serve

hot sauce, to serve

MEATBALLS

2 tablespoons vegetable oil

1 onion, finely chopped

1 garlic clove, crushed

1 teaspoon ground cumin

1 teaspoon ground coriander

½ teaspoon chilli powder

250 g (9 oz) minced (ground) beef

250 g (9 oz) minced (ground) pork

handful of coriander (cilantro), leaves and stalks chopped

CHEESE SAUCE
(MAKES ABOUT 1½ CUPS)

90 g (3 oz/¾ cup) grated tasty cheddar

90 g (3 oz/¾ cup) grated processed cheddar

1 tablespoon cornflour (cornstarch)

125 ml (4 fl oz/½ cup) reduced-fat milk, plus extra if necessary

1 tablespoon chopped pickled jalapeño chilli, or 2 teaspoons hot sauce

For the meatballs, heat half the oil in a large frying pan over medium heat. Add the onion, garlic and spices and cook, stirring, for 6–8 minutes, or until the onion is soft and the spices are fragrant. Remove from the heat.

Combine the beef, pork, coriander and fried onion mixture in a bowl. Season generously with salt and freshly ground black pepper and mix well. Roll level tablespoonfuls of the mixture into balls.

Heat the remaining oil in the same frying pan over medium heat. Working in batches if necessary, cook the meatballs for 6–8 minutes, turning often, until well browned and just cooked through. Season to taste and set aside, covered with foil to keep the meatballs warm.

To make the cheese sauce, toss the cheeses and cornflour in a saucepan until combined. Add the milk and cook over low heat, stirring constantly with a whisk, for about 5 minutes, or until the mixture is melted, smooth and thickened; it should just come to the boil. Add a little more milk to adjust the consistency if necessary. Remove from the heat and stir in the chilli or hot sauce. The cheese sauce may thicken as it cools; if this happens, gently reheat it, adding a little more milk if necessary and stirring until smooth.

Meanwhile, preheat the oven to 170°C (340°F) fan-forced. Spread the tortilla chips over the base of a baking tray or baking dish suitable for serving. Bake for 5 minutes, or until the tortilla chips are lightly toasted.

Drizzle the baked chips with about one-third of the cheese sauce, top with the meatballs and drizzle with the remaining cheese sauce. Add the pico de gallo, scatter with the sliced chilli and coriander, splash with hot sauce and serve immediately.

MEATBALL NACHOS WITH CHEESE SAUCE

CHILAQUILES

SERVES 4

2 tablespoons vegetable oil

1 quantity Roasted tomato salsa (page 16)

1 teaspoon ground cumin

4 eggs

1 quantity Classic tortilla chips (page 10)

queso fresco or crumbled feta, to serve

sliced avocado, to serve

coriander (cilantro), to serve

Crema (page 131) or sour cream, to serve (optional)

Heat half the oil in a large heavy-based frying pan over medium–high heat. Add the salsa, cumin and 80 ml (2½ fl oz/⅓ cup) water and bring to the boil. Reduce the heat to medium and simmer for 4–5 minutes, or until the sauce thickens slightly. Season to taste with salt and freshly ground black pepper.

Meanwhile, heat another frying pan over medium–high heat. Add the remaining oil and cook the eggs to your liking.

Add the tortilla chips to the sauce and stir to coat well. Set aside for a minute or so, until the chips have softened very slightly, but are not mushy.

Divide among serving plates, then top with the fried eggs, cheese, avocado and coriander. Serve immediately, with crema or sour cream if you like.

NOTE

This is one recipe where homemade tortilla chips are really essential; their texture as they soften in the salsa is amazing.

CHILAQUILES

CHICKEN FAJITA NACHOS

SERVES 4

2 teaspoons ground cumin

1 teaspoon smoked hot paprika

1 teaspoon garlic powder

juice and finely grated zest of ½ lime, plus extra lime wedges to serve

2 tablespoons vegetable oil

400 g (14 oz) skinless chicken thigh fillets, cut into thin strips

1 red capsicum (bell pepper), cut into strips

1 red onion, cut into thin wedges

1 quantity Classic tortilla chips (page 10), or 250 g (9 oz) store-bought tortilla chips

250 g (9 oz/2 cups) grated mature cheddar

Smoky bbq sauce (page 60), to serve

Guacamole (page 12), to serve

2 tomatoes, chopped

sour cream, to serve

coriander (cilantro), to serve

Combine the cumin, paprika, garlic powder, lime juice, lime zest and oil in a glass or ceramic bowl. Add the chicken and season with salt and freshly ground black pepper. Toss to combine, then cover and set aside to marinate for 30 minutes, in the refrigerator if the weather is hot.

Preheat a barbecue or chargrill pan to high. Working in batches if necessary, cook the chicken, capsicum and onion, turning occasionally, for 5–6 minutes, or until the vegetables are browned and the chicken is cooked through.

Preheat the oven to 170°C (340°F) fan-forced. Spread half the tortilla chips over the base of a baking tray or baking dish suitable for serving. Scatter with half the cheese, and top with a little less than half the chicken mixture.

Repeat with a second layer of tortilla chips, most of the cheese (reserve some for the top), the remaining chicken mixture and then the remaining cheese.

Bake for 5 minutes, or until the tortilla chips are lightly toasted and the cheese is melted.

Drizzle with bbq sauce, top with guacamole, the chopped tomatoes and sour cream, and scatter with coriander. Serve immediately, with extra bbq sauce on the side.

CHICKEN
FAJITA
NACHOS

PULLED-BEEF CHILLI NACHOS

SERVES 4

1 whole dried ancho chilli, stem and seeds removed

2 whole dried guajillo or pasilla chillies, stems and seeds removed

2 chipotle chillies in adobo sauce, plus 1 tablespoon of the adobo sauce

400 g (14 oz) tin chopped tomatoes

2 tablespoons vegetable oil

1 onion, finely chopped

2 garlic cloves, crushed

3 tablespoons tomato paste (concentrated purée)

2 teaspoons ground cumin

1 teaspoon ground coriander

500 g (1 lb 2 oz) chuck (braising) steak, cut into 5–6 cm (2–2½ inch) chunks

large handful of coriander (cilantro), including the stalks and leaves, chopped separately, plus extra sprigs to serve

1 quantity Classic tortilla chips (page 10), or 250 g (9 oz) store-bought tortilla chips

250 g (9 oz/2 cups) grated mature cheddar

1 quantity Guacamole (page 12), or 1 avocado, chopped

1 quantity Pico de gallo (page 20), or 2 tomatoes, chopped

sour cream, to serve

sliced long red chillies, to serve (optional)

Place the dried ancho and guajillo chillies on a microwave-safe plate and microwave for 10–20 seconds, until pliable and toasty-smelling, or toast in a dry heavy-based frying pan over medium heat until fragrant. Set aside to cool, then crumble the chillies into a blender. Add the chipotle chillies and a few spoonfuls of the tinned tomatoes. Blend until smooth.

Heat the oil in a large heavy-based saucepan over medium heat. Add the onion and garlic and cook for 5 minutes, or until softened. Add the tomato paste, cumin and ground coriander and cook, stirring, for 2 minutes. Add the puréed chilli mixture and the beef. Cook, turning the beef occasionally, for 4–5 minutes, or until the meat has changed colour.

Add the remaining tinned tomatoes, the coriander stalks and enough water to just cover the beef. Stir until combined, then bring to the boil over medium heat. Reduce the heat to low and simmer, uncovered, for 60–70 minutes, or until the beef is tender, adding a little more water if the pan starts to dry out.

Using a slotted spoon, transfer the beef from the pan to a plate. Return the pan to medium–high heat and simmer the sauce for a further 10–15 minutes, until thickened.

Shred the beef with two forks and stir it through the thickened sauce enough to coat the beef generously (you may not need all the sauce). Stir in the chopped coriander leaves and season to taste.

Preheat the oven to 170°C (340°F) fan-forced. Spread half the tortilla chips over the base of a baking tray or baking dish suitable for serving. Scatter with half the cheese, and top with a little less than half the beef mixture.

Repeat with a second layer of tortilla chips, most of the cheese (reserve some for the top), the remaining beef, and then the remaining cheese.

Bake for 5 minutes, or until the tortilla chips are lightly toasted and the cheese is melted. Dollop with the guacamole, pico de gallo and sour cream. Scatter with the extra coriander, and the sliced red chilli if desired. Serve immediately.

PULLED-BEEF CHILLI NACHOS

SERVES 4

2 skinless chicken breast fillets, about 500 g (1 lb 2 oz)

1 onion, chopped

2 teaspoons ground cumin

a good pinch of dried oregano

1 tablespoon vegetable oil

2 garlic cloves, crushed

2 roma (plum) tomatoes, chopped

4 tinned tomatillos, roughly chopped

2 chipotle chillies in adobo sauce, finely chopped, plus extra adobo sauce to taste

1 quantity Classic tortilla chips (page 10), or 250 g (9 oz) store-bought tortilla chips

100 g (3½ oz) marinated goat's cheese or feta, crumbled

small handful of coriander (cilantro), to serve

lime wedges, to serve

PICKLED CABBAGE SLAW

200 g (7 oz) white cabbage, very thinly sliced

½ white onion, very thinly sliced

1 carrot, shredded

½ fresh jalapeño chilli, thinly sliced; if you prefer less heat, remove the seeds and membranes

3 tablespoons apple cider vinegar

1½ teaspoons sugar

¾ teaspoon salt

CHICKEN TINGA

For the slaw, combine the cabbage, onion, carrot and chilli in a bowl. Warm the vinegar, sugar and salt in a small saucepan over medium heat, stirring until the salt and sugar are just dissolved. Pour the brine over the vegetables and toss to combine. Cover and set aside for at least 1 hour before serving; for the best flavour development, make the slaw a few days in advance. It can be refrigerated for up to 1 month in an airtight container.

Cut three deep slashes across the thickest part of each chicken breast. Put the chicken in a heavy-based saucepan with the onion, cumin and oregano. Add enough water to just cover the chicken and stir gently to combine.

Bring to the boil over medium heat, then reduce the heat to low. Cover and simmer for 12–15 minutes, or until the chicken is just cooked through, turning the chicken after 6 minutes.

Transfer the chicken to a cutting board and allow to cool slightly. Strain the solids from the poaching liquid, reserving both.

Heat the oil in the same saucepan and return the strained onion to the pan, along with the garlic. Cook, stirring, for 1–2 minutes, or until fragrant. Add the chopped tomato, tomatillo and chilli. Cook, stirring, for

4–5 minutes, or until the tomato starts to break down. Stir in 185 ml (6 fl oz/¾ cup) of the reserved poaching liquid, bring to the boil, then reduce the heat a little and simmer for 8–10 minutes, or until the sauce has reduced and thickened slightly.

Meanwhile, using two forks, shred the chicken. Return the shredded chicken to the pan and stir for a further minute or so, until the chicken is heated through and evenly coated in the sauce. Season well with salt and freshly ground black pepper, adding a little adobo sauce for extra heat if you like. Keep warm.

Preheat the oven to 170°C (340°F) fan-forced. Spread the tortilla chips over the base of a baking tray or baking dish suitable for serving. Bake for 2–3 minutes, or until the tortilla chips are lightly toasted.

Top the tortilla chips with the chicken mixture. Add the slaw in spoonfuls over the top. Sprinkle the crumbled cheese over, scatter with coriander and serve immediately, with lime wedges.

CHICKEN
TINGA

CHIMICHURRI STEAK NACHOS

SERVES 4

2 x 250 g (9 oz) sirloin steaks

olive oil, for drizzling

1 quantity Classic tortilla chips (page 10), or 250 g (9 oz) store-bought tortilla chips

185 g (6½ oz/1½ cups) grated mature cheddar

marinated soft goat's cheese or feta, to serve

CHIMICHURRI SAUCE

30 g (1 oz/½ cup firmly packed) parsley leaves

small handful of fresh oregano leaves

2 garlic cloves, peeled

½ teaspoon chilli flakes

60 ml (2 fl oz/¼ cup) red wine vinegar

80 ml (2½ fl oz/⅓ cup) olive oil

For the chimichurri sauce, combine the herbs, garlic and chilli flakes in a blender or small food processor and pulse until roughly chopped. Add the vinegar and pulse a few more times. Add the oil and blend until combined. Season to taste with salt and freshly ground black pepper. Transfer to a bowl, cover and set aside, ideally for a few hours, for the flavours to develop.

Season the steaks well with salt and pepper. Heat a barbecue or chargrill pan to high. Drizzle the steaks with a little oil and cook for 5–6 minutes for medium, turning occasionally, until a good crust forms and the steaks are cooked to your liking. Transfer to a warm plate. Spread all over with about 2 tablespoons of the chimichurri sauce, cover lightly with foil and set aside to rest for 5 minutes.

Meanwhile, preheat the oven to 170°C (340°F) fan-forced.

Spread half the tortilla chips over the base of a baking tray or baking dish suitable for serving. Scatter with half the cheddar, then top with the remaining tortilla chips and cheese.

Bake for 5 minutes, or until the tortilla chips are lightly toasted and the cheese is melted.

Slice the steak across the grain into thin strips, and arrange over the baked chips. Drizzle with the remaining chimichurri sauce and scatter with the goat's cheese or feta. Serve immediately.

CHIMICHURRI STEAK NACHOS

PRAWN NACHOS WITH CHARRED PEPPER SALSA

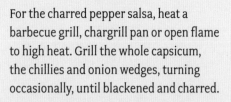

SERVES 4

125 g (4½ oz/½ cup) crème fraîche

2 tablespoons chopped coriander (cilantro)

300 g (10½ oz) peeled raw prawns (shrimp), with tails intact

1 tablespoon vegetable oil

1 teaspoon chilli flakes

1 teaspoon garlic powder

½ teaspoon sweet paprika

1 quantity Classic tortilla chips (page 10), or 250 g (9 oz) store-bought tortilla chips

185 g (6½ oz/1½ cups) grated mature cheddar

lime wedges, to serve

CHARRED PEPPER SALSA

1 red capsicum (bell pepper), left whole

4 fresh jalapeño chillies

2 long red chillies

2 long green chillies

1 red onion, cut into thick wedges

2 tablespoons sherry vinegar

1 tablespoon olive oil

For the charred pepper salsa, heat a barbecue grill, chargrill pan or open flame to high heat. Grill the whole capsicum, the chillies and onion wedges, turning occasionally, until blackened and charred.

Place the charred vegetables in a sealed container and set aside to steam for 15 minutes. Peel the capsicum and chillies, remove the seeds and roughly chop with the onion. Combine in a bowl with the vinegar and olive oil. Season to taste with salt and freshly ground black pepper.

In another small bowl, combine the crème fraîche and coriander. Add 1–2 teaspoons water to thin the mixture to a thick pouring consistency, then season to taste.

Toss the prawns in the oil and spices. Heat a barbecue grill or chargrill pan over high heat. Chargrill the prawns for 1–2 minutes on each side, until charred and just cooked through.

Meanwhile, preheat the oven to 170°C (340°F) fan-forced. Spread half the tortilla chips over the base of a baking dish suitable for serving. Scatter with half the cheese, then top with the remaining tortilla chips and cheese. Bake for 5 minutes, or until the chips are lightly toasted and the cheese is melted.

Top with the prawns and spoonfuls of the salsa. Drizzle with the crème fraîche mixture and serve immediately, with lime wedges.

PRAWN NACHOS WITH CHARRED PEPPER SALSA

PULLED PORK & CHORIZO NACHOS WITH SMOKY BBQ SAUCE

SERVES 4

500 g (1 lb 2 oz) pork scotch fillet (neck), cut into 5 cm (2 inch) chunks

½ teaspoon salt

1 onion, chopped

1 chorizo sausage, about 100 g (3½ oz), skinned and crumbled

400 g (14 oz) tin chopped tomatoes

2 chipotle chillies in adobo sauce, cut into strips, plus 1 tablespoon of the adobo sauce

a pinch each of dried thyme and dried oregano

large handful of coriander (cilantro), including the stalks and leaves, chopped separately

1 quantity Classic tortilla chips (page 10), or 250 g (9 oz) store-bought tortilla chips

250 g (9 oz/2 cups) grated mature cheddar

sour cream, to serve

sliced pickled jalapeño chillies, to serve (optional)

SMOKY BBQ SAUCE (MAKES ABOUT 1 CUP)

400 g (14 oz) tin chopped tomatoes

2 tablespoons brown sugar

1 teaspoon garlic powder

1 teaspoon smoked paprika

60 ml (2 fl oz/¼ cup) maple syrup

1 teaspoon worcestershire sauce

Season the pork with the salt and place in a heavy-based saucepan with the onion. Add just enough water to cover. Bring to the boil over medium heat, then reduce the heat to low and simmer, uncovered, for 40–45 minutes, or until the pork is tender. Remove from the heat and set aside to cool in the broth for 15 minutes. Strain, reserving the stock and solids separately. Shred the pork, discarding any fatty bits, and set aside.

Meanwhile, combine all the smoky bbq sauce ingredients in a saucepan over medium–low heat. Stir until combined, then simmer, stirring occasionally, for 10–15 minutes, or until slightly thickened. Remove from the heat and cool slightly, then purée in a blender or with a hand-held stick blender until smooth. Season to taste with salt and freshly ground black pepper. Use immediately, or store the sauce in an airtight container; it will keep in the refrigerator for up to 2 weeks.

Heat a dry frying pan over low heat. Add the chorizo and cook for 5–6 minutes, or until the fat has rendered out and the sausage is crispy around the edges. Remove from the pan using a slotted spoon and set aside.

Add the strained onion from the stock to the pan, along with the chopped tomato, chipotle chilli and adobo sauce, thyme,

oregano, coriander stalks and 125 ml (4 fl oz/½ cup) of the reserved stock. Cook, uncovered, over medium–high heat for 10–15 minutes, or until thickened.

Stir in the shredded pork and chorizo and cook, stirring occasionally, for a further 2–3 minutes, or until the mixture is juicy but not runny, and is heated through. Add a little more of the pork stock if necessary. Stir in the coriander leaves and season to taste.

Preheat the oven to 170°C (340°F) fan-forced. Spread half the tortilla chips over the base of a baking tray or baking dish. Scatter with half the cheese, then top with about half the pork mixture.

Repeat with a second layer of tortilla chips, most of the cheese (reserve some for the top), the remaining pork, and then the remaining cheese.

Bake for 5 minutes, or until the tortilla chips are lightly toasted and the cheese is melted. Drizzle with the smoky bbq sauce, dollop with sour cream and scatter with jalapeño chilli slices, if using.

Serve immediately, with extra sour cream and smoky bbq sauce on the side.

PULLED PORK & CHORIZO NACHOS WITH SMOKY BBQ SAUCE

STREET CORN NACHOS

SERVES 4

3 corn cobs, husks removed

vegetable oil, for brushing

handful of coriander (cilantro), roughly chopped, plus extra to serve

2 tablespoons pickled jalapeño chillies, chopped, plus 2 tablespoons of the pickling liquid

1 quantity Classic tortilla chips (page 10), or 250 g (9 oz) store-bought tortilla chips

80 g (2¾ oz) cotija or feta cheese, crumbled

1 quantity Roasted tomato salsa (page 16)

1 quantity Crema (page 131), to serve

smoked paprika, for sprinkling (optional)

Heat a chargrill pan or barbecue over high heat. Brush the corn cobs lightly with oil and chargrill for 12–15 minutes, turning occasionally, until lightly charred and cooked. (Alternatively, char over an open flame for 6–8 minutes.) Remove from the heat and set aside until cool enough to handle.

Cut the kernels from the cobs and place them in a bowl. Season lightly with salt and freshly ground black pepper. Add the coriander, chilli and jalapeño pickling liquid and toss together.

Preheat the oven to 170°C (340°F) fan-forced. Spread the tortilla chips over the base of a baking tray or baking dish suitable for serving. Bake for 2–3 minutes, or until the tortilla chips are lightly toasted.

Scatter the warm tortilla chips with the corn mixture. Sprinkle with the crumbled cheese, then drizzle with about half the salsa and half the crema. Add an extra sprinkling of chopped coriander, and a sprinkling of paprika if you like.

Serve immediately, with the remaining salsa and crema.

STREET CORN NACHOS

TEXAS-STYLE CHICKEN NACHOS WITH MANGO & JICAMA SALSA

SERVES 6

½ store-bought barbecued chicken

1 teaspoon ground cumin

1 teaspoon ground coriander

handful of coriander (cilantro), chopped, plus extra to serve

60 ml (2 fl oz/¼ cup) chicken stock or water

½ quantity Classic tortilla chips (page 10), or 150 g (5½ oz) good-quality round tortilla chips

150 g (5½ oz/1¼ cups) grated mature cheddar

chopped almonds, to serve

MANGO & JICAMA SALSA

1 small mango cheek, flesh finely cubed

½ small jicama, peeled and finely cubed

zest and juice of ½ lime

CORIANDER & MINT PESTO

30 g (1 oz/½ cup, tightly packed) coriander (cilantro), roughly chopped, plus extra to serve

2 tablespoons mint leaves, roughly chopped

½ small garlic clove, crushed

3 tablespoons almonds

2 tablespoons lime juice

60 ml (2 fl oz/¼ cup) vegetable oil

Combine all the salsa ingredients in a small bowl. Season lightly with salt and set aside.

To make the coriander and mint pesto, whiz the coriander, mint, garlic and almonds in a small food processor or blender until finely chopped. With the motor operating, add the lime juice and oil in a thin, steady stream until combined, thinning the pesto down with a little water if necessary. Season to taste with salt and freshly ground black pepper.

Preheat the oven to 170°C (340°F) fan-forced. Remove the meat from the chicken and shred it using two forks. Toss the chicken with the ground spices, chopped coriander and enough stock or water to just moisten the chicken. Season well.

Spread the tortilla chips in a single layer over two baking trays. Top each tortilla chip with a little pile of chicken mixture, then top each with cheese.

Bake for 5 minutes, or until the tortilla chips are lightly toasted and the cheese is melted.

Remove from the oven and top each chip with a small spoonful of the salsa, scatter with the chopped almonds, extra coriander and a drizzle of pesto. Serve immediately.

NOTE

If jicama is unavailable, use ½ finely cubed, peeled and seeded Lebanese (short) or small green cucumber.

TEXAS-STYLE CHICKEN NACHOS WITH MANGO & JICAMA SALSA

NEW CLASSICS

BREAKFAST NACHOS WITH CHIPOTLE HOLLANDAISE

SERVES 4

1 tablespoon olive oil

4 bacon rashers (slices), about 200 g (7 oz), cut into thick strips

2 tablespoons maple syrup

1 quantity Classic tortilla chips (page 10), or 250 g (9 oz) store-bought tortilla chips

4 eggs

1 quantity Refried beans (page 14), warmed

1 baby cos (romaine) lettuce, roughly chopped

1 avocado, sliced, to serve

coriander (cilantro), to serve

CHIPOTLE HOLLANDAISE

3 egg yolks

1 tablespoon lime juice

60 g (2 oz) butter, cut into 1.5 cm (½ inch) cubes, softened

2 teaspoons chopped coriander (cilantro)

½ chipotle chilli in adobo sauce, chopped, plus 1 teaspoon of the adobo sauce

For the hollandaise, whisk the egg yolks and lime juice in a large heatproof bowl. Place the bowl over a saucepan of simmering water over low heat; the bowl should fit snugly over the top of the pan, and should not touch the water. Whisk for 3 minutes, or until the mixture becomes thick and pale. Add the butter one cube at a time, whisking until melted before adding the next; this may take 6–8 minutes. Remove from the heat. Stir in the coriander, chilli and adobo sauce, then season to taste with salt and freshly ground black pepper. Sit in a warm spot, covered, until ready to serve, whisking occasionally. The hollandaise should hold for 30 minutes or so; if needed, you can thin it out by whisking in a little warm water just before serving.

Preheat the oven to 170°C (340°F) fan-forced.

Meanwhile, heat the oil in a heavy-based frying pan over medium–high heat and cook the bacon, stirring often, for 4–5 minutes, or until cooked through and slightly crispy. Add the maple syrup and stir for a further minute or two, until the bacon is glossy.

Spread half the tortilla chips over the base of heatproof dishes or plates, or a baking tray or baking dish suitable for serving. Drizzle with half the hollandaise, then top with the remaining tortilla chips. Bake for 5 minutes, or until the tortilla chips are lightly toasted.

Meanwhile, poach or fry the eggs.

Top the baked chips with the refried beans, eggs and bacon. Drizzle with the remaining hollandaise, scatter with lettuce, avocado slices and coriander. Serve immediately.

BREAKFAST NACHOS WITH CHIPOTLE HOLLANDAISE

CHEESEBOARD NACHOS

SERVES 4

1 quantity Classic tortilla chips (page 10), or 250 g (9 oz) store-bought tortilla chips

125 g (4½ oz/1 cup) grated mature cheddar

120 g (4½ oz) brie, sliced

50 g (1¾ oz) feta, crumbled

50 g (1¾ oz) creamy blue cheese, torn into small pieces

handful of toasted walnuts, roughly chopped, to serve

handful of dried cranberries, to serve

3 baby radishes, very thinly sliced, to serve

sorrel leaves, to serve

Preheat the oven to 170°C (340°F) fan-forced.

Spread half the tortilla chips over the base of four heatproof dishes or plates, or a large baking tray or baking dish suitable for serving. Top with about half the cheddar and half the brie, then repeat the layers with the remaining tortilla chips, cheddar and brie.

Bake for 5 minutes, or until the tortilla chips are lightly toasted and the cheese is melted.

Top with the feta and blue cheese and scatter with the walnuts, cranberries, radish slices and sorrel leaves. Serve immediately.

CHEESEBOARD
NACHOS

BRUSCHETTA NACHOS WITH KALE CRISPS

SERVES 4

1 large garlic clove, halved lengthways

1 quantity Classic tortilla chips (page 10), or 250 g (9 oz) store-bought tortilla chips

500 g (1 lb 2 oz) perfectly ripe mixed heirloom tomatoes

large handful of basil leaves

2 tablespoons extra virgin olive oil

2 tablespoons red wine vinegar or sherry vinegar

150 g (5½ oz) fresh ricotta

KALE CRISPS

½ bunch Tuscan kale, about 175 g (6 oz)

1 tablespoon olive oil

2 garlic cloves, thinly sliced

1 teaspoon sweet paprika

½ teaspoon sea salt flakes

Preheat the oven to 160°C (320°F) fan-forced.

For the kale crisps, trim the tough stems from the kale and tear any larger leaves in half. Wash well, then dry using a salad spinner or clean dry cloth.

Put the kale in a large bowl and drizzle with the oil. Mix well with your hands, ensuring the leaves are well coated all over. Spread the kale in a single layer over a large baking tray. Sprinkle with the garlic, paprika and salt.

Bake for 12–15 minutes, or until the leaves are crisp. Remove from the oven and set aside.

Increase the oven temperature to 170°C (340°F) fan-forced. Rub the cut side of the garlic clove gently over the surface of the tortilla chips.

Cut the tomatoes in half horizontally and squeeze out the seeds. Roughly chop the tomatoes and place in a bowl. Gently tear the basil into the bowl, add the oil and vinegar and toss well to combine. Season to taste with salt and freshly ground black pepper.

Spread the tortilla chips over the base of four heatproof dishes or plates, or over a large baking tray or baking dish suitable for serving. Bake for 2–3 minutes, or until the tortilla chips are lightly toasted.

Crumble the ricotta over the warm chips and top with the tomato mixture. Scatter with the kale crisps and serve.

83

BRUSCHETTA NACHOS WITH KALE CRISPS

BUFFALO CHICKEN NACHOS

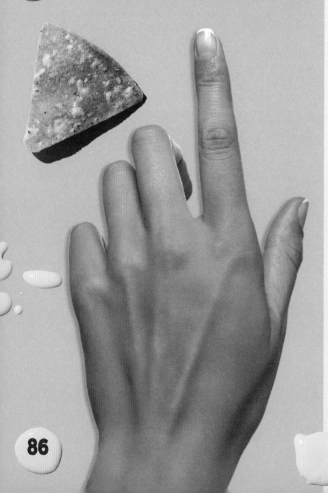

SERVES 4

50 g (1¾ oz/⅓ cup) plain (all-purpose) flour

2 teaspoons garlic powder

1 teaspoon salt

1 teaspoon smoked hot paprika

400 g (14 oz) skinless chicken thigh fillets, cut into 2 cm (¾ inch) wide strips

olive oil spray, for cooking

1 quantity Classic tortilla chips (page 10), or 250 g (9 oz) store-bought tortilla chips

250 g (9 oz/2 cups) grated mature cheddar

60 ml (2 fl oz/¼ cup) hot sauce, such as Cholula

40 g (1½ oz) butter, melted

2 celery stalks, very thinly sliced on the diagonal

BLUE CHEESE SAUCE

150 g (5½ oz) blue cheese

1 small garlic clove, crushed

100 g (3½ oz/⅓ cup) whole-egg mayonnaise

60 g (2 oz/¼ cup) sour cream

4 teaspoons lemon juice, or to taste

ground white pepper, to taste

For the blue cheese sauce, mash the cheese and garlic together in a bowl using a fork until smooth. Whisk in the mayonnaise, sour cream and lemon juice until well combined. (Alternatively, you can blend the ingredients if you prefer a silky-smooth sauce.) Season to taste with salt and ground white pepper. Cover and refrigerate until required.

Preheat the oven to 220°C (430°F) fan-forced. Combine the flour, garlic powder, salt and paprika in a bag or container. Add the chicken, then seal the bag and shake to coat the chicken well. Remove the chicken from the bag or container, shake off the excess flour and place on a wire rack, set over a baking tray. Spray lightly with olive oil spray.

Roast for 20–25 minutes, or until the chicken is crisp and cooked through. Remove from the oven and cover lightly with foil to keep warm.

Reduce the oven temperature to 170°C (340°F). Spread half the tortilla chips over the base of four heatproof dishes or plates, or a large baking tray or baking dish suitable for serving. Top with half the cheese, then repeat the layers with the remaining tortilla chips and cheese.

Bake for 5 minutes, or until the tortilla chips are lightly toasted and the cheese is melted.

Meanwhile, whisk the hot sauce and butter together in a bowl. Just before serving, add the hot chicken and stir gently to combine.

As soon as the tortilla chips come out of the oven, top with the chicken and drizzle with the blue cheese sauce. Scatter with the celery and serve immediately, with any left-over cheese sauce and hot butter sauce on the side.

NOTE

If blue cheese sauce is not your favourite thing, sour cream works really well as an alternative.

BUFFALO CHICKEN NACHOS

CHEESE
BURGER
NACHOS

SERVES 4–6

1 tablespoon vegetable oil

1 onion, chopped

2 tablespoons tomato paste (concentrated purée)

2 garlic cloves, crushed

250 g (9 oz) minced (ground) beef

250 g (9 oz) minced (ground) pork

3 tablespoons barbecue sauce

1 quantity Classic tortilla chips (page 10), or 250 g (9 oz) store-bought tortilla chips

1 quantity Cheese sauce (page 32), warmed

sliced dill pickles, to serve

tomato sauce or ketchup, to serve

MUSTARD AÏOLI

150 g (5½ oz/½ cup) homemade or good-quality mayonnaise

4 teaspoons American-style mustard

1 garlic clove, crushed

Preheat the oven to 170°C (340°F) fan-forced. Heat the oil in a frying pan over medium–low heat and cook the onion, stirring often, for 5–6 minutes, or until softened. Add the tomato paste and garlic and cook, stirring, for 2 minutes, or until fragrant. Increase the heat to medium–high and add the beef and pork. Cook, stirring, for 6–8 minutes, or until the meat is well browned and starting to stick to the base of the pan. Stir in the barbecue sauce and season to taste.

Combine the mustard aïoli ingredients in a small bowl, mixing well. Set aside.

Spread half the tortilla chips over the base of a baking tray or baking dish suitable for serving. Drizzle with half the cheese sauce, then top with a little less than half the meat mixture. Add the remaining tortilla chips and top with the remaining meat mixture. Bake for 5 minutes, or until the tortilla chips are lightly toasted.

Drizzle with the remaining cheese sauce. Top with the pickles, a splash of tomato sauce or ketchup, and the mustard aïoli. Serve immediately.

NOTES

For a quicker option, use 185 g (6½ oz/1½ cups) grated mature cheddar instead of the cheese sauce. Sprinkle half over the tortilla chips, then scatter most of the remaining cheese over the second layer of tortilla chips, sprinkling the rest of the cheese over the final dish.

If you like, you can add a scattering of crispy bacon, or serve the nachos with a little shredded lettuce and chopped tomato.

CHEESE BURGER NACHOS

SAUSAGE NACHOS WITH 4-CHEESE BEER SAUCE

SERVES 4–6

200 g (7 oz) kransky or other European-style smoked sausage, sliced

1 quantity Classic tortilla chips (page 10), or 250 g (9 oz) store-bought tortilla chips

1 spring onion (scallion), thinly sliced

sliced dill pickles, to serve

4-CHEESE BEER SAUCE

60 g (2 oz/½ cup) grated smoked or vintage cheddar

60 g (2 oz/½ cup) grated raclette cheese

60 g (2 oz/½ cup) grated processed cheese

2 tablespoons cornflour (cornstarch)

100 g (3½ oz) camembert, rind on

125 ml (4 fl oz/½ cup) German beer, any variety

2 spring onions (scallions), chopped

Preheat the oven to 170°C (340°F) fan-forced.

Heat a dry frying pan over medium heat. Cook the sausage for 5–6 minutes, or until golden and a little crispy around the edges. Remove from the pan using a slotted spoon and drain on paper towel.

To make the cheese sauce, toss the three grated cheeses in a saucepan with the cornflour until combined. Depending on the ripeness of the camembert, chop or mash it (including the rind), then add to the pan and toss to combine. Stir in most of the beer. Cook over low heat, whisking gently and constantly, for about 5 minutes, or until the mixture is melted and smooth; it should come to the boil and bubble gently for 30 seconds or so. Remove from the heat and stir in the spring onion. The cheese sauce may thicken as it cools; if this happens, gently reheat it, adding a little more beer if necessary and stirring until smooth.

Meanwhile, spread the tortilla chips over the base of four heatproof serving dishes, a baking tray or baking dish suitable for serving. Bake for 5 minutes, or until the tortilla chips are lightly toasted.

Remove the toasted chips from the oven. Working quickly, remove about half the chips and place them in a warm bowl for a moment. Drizzle the remaining baked chips with about half the cheese sauce, top with about half the crispy sausage, then the remaining tortilla chips and sausage.

Drizzle with the remaining cheese sauce, scatter with the spring onion and dill pickles, and serve immediately.

SAUSAGE NACHOS WITH 4-CHEESE BEER SAUCE

DIRTY MAC & CHEESE NACHOS

SERVES 4

260 g (9 oz/about 1 cup) left-over Pulled pork (page 60), Pulled beef (page 44) or Chicken tinga (page 48)

handful of coriander (cilantro), including the stalks and leaves, chopped, plus extra to serve

1 quantity Classic tortilla chips (page 10), or 250 g (9 oz) store-bought tortilla chips

15 g (½ oz/¼ cup) panko breadcrumbs

1 tablespoon softened butter

hot sauce, to serve

MAC & CHEESE

150 g (5½ oz) dried macaroni

30 g (1 oz) butter

2 tablespoons plain (all-purpose) flour

250 ml (8½ fl oz/1 cup) full-cream (whole) milk

125 g (4½ oz/1 cup) grated cheese; use a combination of tasty cheddar and gruyère or Swiss cheese

Preheat the oven to 170°C (340°F) fan-forced.

For the mac and cheese, cook the macaroni in a saucepan of boiling water according to the packet directions until al dente. Drain the pasta and return to the pan.

Meanwhile, melt the butter in a saucepan over medium–low heat and add the flour. Cook, stirring, for about 1 minute, until bubbling. Gradually add the milk, whisking until smooth. Stir until the mixture comes to the boil, then reduce the heat and simmer for 2 minutes. Remove from the heat, add the cheese and stir until melted and smooth. Season to taste.

When the macaroni is cooked, pour the cheese sauce over the pasta. Add the pork, beef or chicken, sprinkle with the coriander and fold together until only just combined. Don't over-mix — there should be pockets of mac and cheese, and pockets of the meat mixture.

Spread half the tortilla chips over the base of a baking tray or baking dish suitable for serving. Spoon over half the mac and cheese mixture. Repeat with a second layer of tortilla chips and the remaining mac and cheese. Gently rub the breadcrumbs and butter together with your fingertips and scatter over the top.

Bake for 8–10 minutes, or until the tortilla chips are lightly toasted and the mixture is heated through.

Drizzle with hot sauce and extra coriander and serve immediately.

NOTE

You can pop the nachos under a hot grill (broiler) for a minute or so, to brown the crumbs if necessary.

To freshen it up, you can serve the nachos topped with lettuce, tomato, avocado and sliced jalapeño chillies if you like, although it is dirty and delicious as is.

DIRTY MAC & CHEESE NACHOS

KOREAN CHICKEN NACHOS

SERVES 4

2 tablespoons gochujang (Korean chilli paste)

1 tablespoon soy sauce

1 tablespoon sesame oil

400 g (14 oz) skinless chicken thigh fillets

1 tablespoon vegetable oil

1 quantity Classic tortilla chips (page 10), or 250 g (9 oz) store-bought tortilla chips

1 quantity Garlic aïoli (page 18) or sour cream

240 g (8½ oz/1 cup) kimchi

1 spring onion (scallion), thinly sliced

2 teaspoons roasted black sesame seeds

Mix the gochujang, soy sauce and sesame oil in a small bowl until well combined. Add the chicken, then cover and marinate at room temperature for 30 minutes. (Alternatively, you can marinate the chicken in the refrigerator for a few hours, or overnight.)

Preheat the oven to 170°C (340°F) fan-forced.

Heat the vegetable oil in a heavy-based frying pan or chargrill pan over medium–high heat. Cook the chicken for 10–12 minutes, or until cooked through, turning occasionally. Set aside, covered with foil to rest and keep warm.

Spread the tortilla chips over the base of four heatproof dishes or plates, or a baking tray or baking dish suitable for serving. Bake for 3–4 minutes, or until the tortilla chips are lightly toasted.

Slice the chicken. Drizzle the tortilla chips generously with aïoli, top with the chicken and dollop with spoonfuls of the kimchi. Drizzle with more aïoli and scatter with the spring onion and sesame seeds. Serve immediately, with any remaining aïoli.

KOREAN CHICKEN NACHOS

ROAST VEG NACHOS WITH FETA DRESSING

SERVES 4

1 quantity Classic tortilla chips (page 10), or 250 g (9 oz) store-bought tortilla chips

250 g (9 oz/2 cups) grated mature cheddar

50 g (1¾ oz/⅓ cup) large pimento-stuffed olive halves

ROAST VEGETABLES

1 orange sweet potato, about 400 g (14 oz), unpeeled, scrubbed and chopped into 2 cm (¾ inch) chunks

1 red capsicum (bell pepper), cut into 3 cm (1¼ inch) chunks

1 zucchini (courgette), cut into 3 cm (1¼ inch) chunks

400 g (14 oz) tin chickpeas, drained

1 small red onion, cut into thin wedges

4 garlic cloves, lightly bruised

1 rosemary sprig, leaves stripped

1 tablespoon olive oil

1 tablespoon balsamic vinegar

FETA DRESSING

100 g (3½ oz) feta

1 teaspoon dijon mustard

1 teaspoon finely chopped fresh oregano, thyme or parsley

2 tablespoons white wine vinegar

2 tablespoons olive oil

Preheat the oven to 200°C (400°C) fan-forced. Toss all the ingredients for the roast vegetables together in a large roasting tin until well combined. Season well with salt and freshly ground black pepper. Roast for 25–30 minutes, or until the vegetables are tender and browned around the edges.

Meanwhile, make the feta dressing. Using a fork, mash the feta with the mustard, herbs and vinegar until fairly smooth. Add the oil and 45 ml (1½ fl oz) water and whisk until smooth. (Alternatively, you can blend the ingredients together if you prefer a silky-smooth sauce.) Season to taste.

Reduce the oven temperature to 170°C (340°F) fan-forced.

Spread half the tortilla chips over the base of a baking tray or baking dish suitable for serving. Scatter with half the cheddar and top with about half the roasted vegetable mixture. Repeat with a second layer of tortilla chips, most of the cheddar (reserve some for the top), the remaining vegetable mixture and then the remaining cheddar.

Bake for 5 minutes, or until the tortilla chips are lightly toasted and the cheese is melted. Top with the olives. Serve immediately, with the feta dressing on the side.

ROAST VEG NACHOS WITH FETA DRESSING

PIMENTO CHEESE & CHORIZO NACHOS

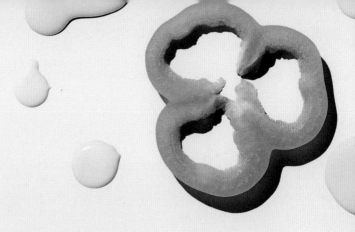

SERVES 4

1 red or yellow capsicum (bell pepper), quartered

1 quantity Classic tortilla chips (page 10), or 250 g (9 oz) store-bought tortilla chips

1 chorizo sausage, about 100 g (3½ oz), cut into 1 cm (½ inch) pieces

handful of coriander (cilantro), to serve

PIMENTO CHEESE

250 g (9 oz/2 cups) grated mature cheddar

120 g (4½ oz/½ cup) pimento or other roasted red peppers, well drained and finely chopped

100 g (3½ oz/⅓ cup) good-quality mayonnaise

¼ small onion, finely chopped

2 teaspoons hot sauce

Preheat the oven grill (broiler) to high heat. Line a baking tray with foil. Place the capsicum, skin side up, on the tray and grill for 8–10 minutes, or until well charred and softened. (Alternatively roast the capsicum over a flame until well charred.) Transfer to a bowl, cover with plastic wrap and set aside to sweat for 15 minutes. Peel off and discard the skin, then cut the capsicum into strips.

Combine the pimento cheese ingredients in a bowl. Season to taste with salt and pepper. Use immediately, or store in an airtight container in the refrigerator for up to 1 week.

Preheat the oven to 170°C (340°F) fan-forced. Spread half the tortilla chips over the base of a baking tray or baking dish suitable for serving. Spoon a little less than half the pimento cheese over the top. Repeat with a second layer of tortilla chips and the remaining pimento cheese.

Bake for 5 minutes, or until the tortilla chips are lightly toasted and the cheese is melted. Meanwhile, heat a dry frying pan over medium–low heat. Cook the chorizo for 5 minutes, or until browned and a little crispy around the edges. Remove from the pan using a slotted spoon and drain on paper towel.

Top the hot nachos immediately with the roasted capsicum and chorizo. Scatter with the coriander and serve.

PIMENTO CHEESE & CHORIZO NACHOS

PIZZA
NACHOS

SERVES 4

1 quantity Classic tortilla chips (page 10), or 250 g (9 oz) store-bought tortilla chips

300 g (10½ oz/2 cups) grated mozzarella

260 g (9 oz/1 cup) store-bought Napoli sauce or tomato salsa

120 g (4½ oz) sliced pepperoni

½ red onion, thinly sliced

dried oregano, for sprinkling

60 g (2 oz/½ cup) sliced olives

handful of basil leaves

pinch of chilli flakes, to serve (optional)

anchovies, to serve (optional)

Preheat the oven to 170°C (340°F) fan-forced.

Spread half the tortilla chips over the base of a baking tray or baking dish suitable for serving. Scatter with half the cheese. Top with about half the sauce or salsa, half the pepperoni and half the onion. Sprinkle with half the oregano.

Add a layer of the remaining tortilla chips, then most of the cheese (reserve some for the top), the remaining sauce or salsa, and the remaining pepperoni, onion and oregano. Scatter with the remaining cheese.

Bake for 5 minutes, or until the tortilla chips are lightly toasted and the cheese is melted.

Top with the olives and basil, and scatter with the chilli flakes and anchovies, if using. Serve immediately.

PIZZA NACHOS

PRAWN & CRAB NACHOS

SERVES 4

300 g (10½ oz) peeled raw prawns (shrimp), with tails intact

2 tablespoons chopped coriander (cilantro), plus extra to serve

2 garlic cloves, crushed

1 teaspoon Cajun spice mix

1 tablespoon vegetable oil

180 g (6½ oz/¾ cup) sour cream

4 spring onions (scallions), thinly sliced

150 g (5½ oz) crab meat pieces

1 quantity Classic tortilla chips (page 10), or 250 g (9 oz) store-bought tortilla chips

185 g (6½ oz/1½ cups) grated mature cheddar

1 avocado, sliced

pickled sliced jalapeño chillies, to serve

Preheat the oven to 170°C (340°F) fan-forced.

Toss the prawns in a bowl with the coriander, garlic, spice mix and oil. Heat a barbecue grill, chargrill pan or large frying pan over high heat. Chargrill the prawns for 1–2 minutes on each side, or until charred and just cooked through. Remove from the heat.

Combine the sour cream and spring onion in a bowl. Add the grilled prawns and crab meat and toss gently to combine. Season to taste with salt and freshly ground black pepper.

Spread half the tortilla chips over the base of a baking tray or baking dish suitable for serving. Scatter with half the cheese. Top with the remaining tortilla chips, most of the cheese (reserve some for the top), the prawn mixture, and then the remaining cheese.

Bake for 5 minutes, or until the tortilla chips are lightly toasted and the cheese is melted.

Top with the avocado and scatter with the chilli and extra coriander. Serve immediately.

PRAWN & CRAB NACHOS

TOP-SHELF NACHOS

SERVES 4

60 g (2 oz) prosciutto slices

15 g (½ oz) butter

1 tablespoon olive oil

1 large leek, trimmed, very well washed and thinly sliced

a pinch of salt

2 garlic cloves, thinly sliced

1 quantity Classic tortilla chips (page 10), or 250 g (9 oz) store-bought tortilla chips

200 g (7 oz) brie, sliced

handful of rocket (arugula), to serve

1 pear, cored and thinly sliced, to serve

handful of toasted hazelnuts, roughly chopped, to serve

honey, for drizzling

Preheat the oven to 170°C (340°F) fan-forced.

Heat a large heavy-based frying pan over medium–high heat. Add the prosciutto to the dry frying pan and cook for 1–2 minutes, turning occasionally, until crisp. Drain on paper towel. Break into large pieces and set aside.

Reduce the heat to medium and add the butter and oil to the same pan. Add the leek and a good pinch of salt and cook for 8–10 minutes, or until tender, stirring occasionally. Add the garlic and cook, stirring, for 1–2 minutes, or until fragrant.

Spread half the tortilla chips over the base of four heatproof dishes or plates, or a large baking tray or baking dish suitable for serving. Top with half the leek mixture and half the brie, then repeat the layers with the remaining tortilla chips, leek and brie.

Bake for 5 minutes, or until the tortilla chips are lightly toasted and the brie is melted.

Scatter with the rocket, pear and hazelnuts, drizzle with honey and top with the crispy prosciutto. Serve immediately.

TOP-SHELF
NACHOS

VEGAN LOADED NACHOS

SERVES 4

1 quantity Classic tortilla chips (page 10), or 250 g (9 oz) store-bought tortilla chips

1 quantity Refried beans (page 14)

400 g (14 oz) tin black beans, drained

185 g (6½ oz/1½ cups) vegan cheddar, grated

1 quantity Pico de gallo (page 20)

1 avocado, sliced

1 baby cos (romaine) lettuce, shredded

3 baby radishes, very thinly sliced

handful of pepitas (pumpkin seeds), toasted

coriander (cilantro), to serve

lime wedges, to serve

Preheat the oven to 170°C (340°F) fan-forced.

Spread the tortilla chips over the base of a baking tray or baking dish suitable for serving. Bake for 5 minutes, or until the tortilla chips are lightly toasted.

Meanwhile, warm the refried beans gently in a saucepan over medium heat, stirring in a splash of water to loosen the mixture if necessary.

Top the baked chips with dollops of the refried beans and scatter with the black beans. Sprinkle with the cheese and top with the pico de gallo, avocado, lettuce, radish, pepitas and coriander.

Serve immediately, with the lime wedges.

VEGAN
LOADED
NACHOS

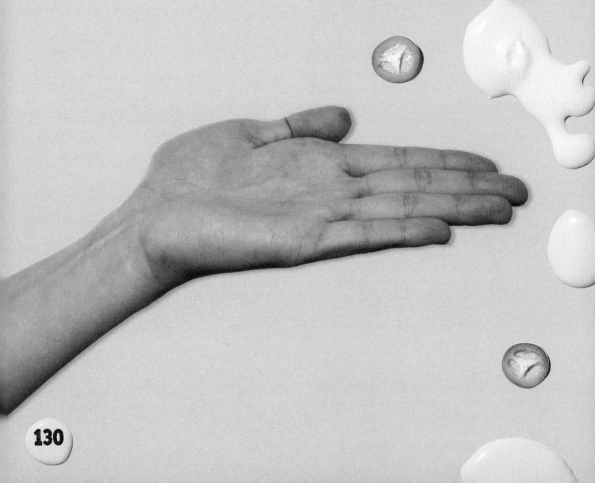

SALMON CEVICHE NACHOS

SERVES 4

300 g (10½ oz) sashimi-quality skinless salmon fillet, pin-boned

80 ml (2½ fl oz/⅓ cup) lime juice

1 quantity Classic tortilla chips (page 10)

200 g (7 oz) cherry tomatoes, some halved, the others quartered

1 small green or Lebanese (short) cucumber, chopped

1 avocado, sliced

handful of coriander (cilantro), roughly chopped, plus extra to serve

handful of mint leaves, roughly chopped, plus extra to serve

1 tablespoon pickled jalapeño chillies, chopped

lime wedges, to serve

CREMA

125 g (4½ oz/½ cup) crème fraîche or sour cream

2 tablespoons lime juice

Cut the salmon into 1 cm (½ inch) pieces and place in a glass or ceramic bowl. Add the lime juice, stir gently to coat the salmon well, then cover and marinate in the refrigerator for 30 minutes.

Meanwhile, prepare the homemade tortillas, and scatter them over a serving platter or individual serving plates.

For the crema, combine the crème fraîche or sour cream and lime juice in a small bowl. Mix well and add a little salt to taste. Stir in a little more lime juice or a few drops of water, for a thick pourable consistency.

Remove the salmon from the refrigerator and drain off any excess lime juice. Add the tomato, cucumber, avocado, chopped herbs and chilli. Toss gently to combine. Season lightly with salt and freshly ground black pepper.

Spoon the salmon mixture over the tortilla chips. Drizzle with the crema, scatter with extra herbs and serve immediately, with lime wedges.

NOTE

This recipe is also good served on individual tortilla chips.

SALMON CEVICHE NACHOS

LENTIL & ROASTED TOMATO NACHOS WITH CORN SALSA

SERVES 4

4 roma (plum) tomatoes, cored

1 tablespoon vegetable oil

1 onion, chopped

2 tablespoons tomato paste (concentrated purée)

2 teaspoons ground cumin

1 teaspoon ground coriander

2 garlic cloves, crushed

200 g (7 oz) Swiss brown mushrooms, finely chopped

1 zucchini (courgette), finely chopped

large handful of coriander (cilantro), chopped, plus extra to serve

400 g (14 oz) tin brown lentils, drained

1 quantity Classic tortilla chips (page 10), or 250 g (9 oz) store-bought tortilla chips

250 g (9 oz/2 cups) grated mature cheddar

sour cream, to serve

GRILLED CORN SALSA

1 corn cob, husk removed

vegetable oil, for brushing

small handful of coriander (cilantro), chopped

1 French shallot, thinly sliced

1 tablespoon pickled sliced jalapeño chillies, chopped, plus 1 tablespoon of the pickling liquid

1 tablespoon lime juice

Preheat the oven to 180°C (350°F) fan-forced. Roast the tomatoes in a roasting tin for 25–30 minutes, or until starting to collapse and slightly charred in spots. Remove from the oven and set aside to cool slightly. Remove and discard the skins. Chop the tomatoes roughly, retaining all the juices. Season to taste with salt if necessary.

Heat the oil in a large frying pan over medium–low heat and cook the onion, stirring often, for 5–6 minutes, or until softened. Add the tomato paste, cumin, ground coriander and garlic and cook, stirring, for 2 minutes. Increase the heat to medium–high and add the mushroom, zucchini and a good pinch of salt. Cook, stirring, for 6–8 minutes, or until softened.

Stir in the chopped roasted tomato, coriander stalks, lentils and 125 ml (4 fl oz/½ cup) water. Bring to the boil, reduce the heat and simmer, uncovered, for 4–5 minutes, or until slightly thickened. Stir in the coriander leaves and season to taste with salt and freshly ground black pepper.

Meanwhile, for the grilled corn salsa, heat a chargrill pan over high heat. Brush the corn cob lightly with oil and chargrill for 12–15 minutes, turning occasionally, until lightly charred and cooked. (Alternatively, char the corn over an open flame for 6–8 minutes.) Remove from the heat and set aside to cool.

Cut the kernels from the cob and place in a bowl. Stir in the remaining salsa ingredients and set aside at room temperature for the flavours to develop. Season to taste.

Reduce the oven temperature to 170°C (340°F) fan-forced. Spread half the tortilla chips over the base of a baking tray or baking dish suitable for serving. Scatter with half the cheese and top with about half the lentil mixture.

Repeat with a second layer of tortilla chips, most of the cheese (reserve some for the top), the remaining lentil mixture, and then the remaining cheese.

Bake for 7–8 minutes, or until the tortilla chips are lightly toasted and the cheese is melted. Top with the corn salsa, sour cream and extra coriander. Serve immediately.

**LENTIL &
ROASTED
TOMATO
NACHOS WITH
CORN SALSA**

CARAMELISED APPLE DESSERT NACHOS

SERVES 4–6

170 g (6 oz/¾ cup) caster (superfine) sugar

2 teaspoons ground cinnamon

250 g (9 oz) store-bought tortilla chips, or 1 quantity Classic tortilla chips (page 10)

80 g (2¾ oz) butter, if using store-bought tortilla chips

thick (double/heavy) cream, sour cream or ice cream, to serve

toasted sesame seeds, for sprinkling

CARAMELISED APPLE

80 g (2¾ oz) butter

80 g (2¾ oz/⅓ cup, firmly packed) brown sugar

4 granny smith apples, unpeeled, cut into 1 cm (½ inch) pieces

4 teaspoons vanilla bean paste

For the caramelised apple, melt the butter in a saucepan over medium heat. Add the sugar, apple and vanilla bean paste, and cook, stirring, until the sugar dissolves. Cook, stirring occasionally, for a further 5–6 minutes, or until the apple is tender and the liquid slightly thickened.

Meanwhile, combine the caster sugar and cinnamon in a large bowl.

For store-bought tortilla chips, preheat the oven to 170°C (340°F) fan-forced. Melt the butter and pour into a large bowl. Add the tortilla chips and toss until well coated in the butter. Working in batches, toss the chips in the cinnamon sugar. Spread the sugar-coated tortilla chips over a baking tray or baking dish suitable for serving. Bake for 5 minutes, or until the chips are warmed through and lightly toasted.

Top the store-bought tortilla chips with the warm caramelised apple mixture and cream, and scatter with the sesame seeds. Serve immediately.

If using homemade tortilla chips, toss the hot chips in the cinnamon sugar immediately after cooking them. There is no need to bake them, simply top with the warm caramelised apple mixture and other toppings and serve immediately.

CARAMELISED
APPLE DESSERT
NACHOS

DESSERT NACHOS WITH CINNAMON & ORANGE ICE CREAM

SERVES 4–6

170 g (6 oz/¾ cup) caster (superfine) sugar

1 teaspoon ground cinnamon

½ teaspoon ground star anise

250 g (9 oz) store-bought tortilla chips, or 1 quantity Classic tortilla chips (page 10)

80 g (2¾ oz) butter, if using store-bought tortilla chips

shredded orange zest, to serve

CINNAMON & ORANGE ICE CREAM (MAKES ABOUT 1 LITRE/34 FL OZ/4 CUPS)

500 ml (17 fl oz/2 cups) full-cream (whole) milk

250 ml (8½ fl oz/1 cup) cream (35% fat)

3 cinnamon sticks, broken

1 tablespoon finely grated orange zest

2 teaspoons vanilla bean paste

1 tablespoon orange-flavoured liqueur (optional)

5 extra-large free-range egg yolks

155 g (5½ oz/⅔ cup, firmly packed) brown sugar

MEXICAN CHOCOLATE SAUCE

180 ml (6 fl oz) cream (35% fat)

180 g (6½ oz) dark chocolate, chopped

½ teaspoon ground cinnamon

To make the ice cream, pour the milk and cream into a heavy-based saucepan and add the cinnamon sticks. Cook, stirring constantly, over medium–low heat, until the mixture only just comes to the boil. Remove from the heat, cover and set aside to infuse for 30 minutes.

Strain the milk mixture, discarding the cinnamon, and stir in the orange zest, vanilla bean paste and liqueur, if using. Whisk the egg yolks and sugar in a large bowl until thickened. Gradually whisk in the warm milk mixture, then pour back into the saucepan. Place the pan over medium heat and cook, stirring constantly, until the mixture thickens slightly and coats the back of a spoon (85°C/185°F on a sugar thermometer).

Pour the ice cream custard mixture into a large bowl set over an ice bath and stir until cold. Cover and refrigerate for about 4 hours, or preferably overnight, until thoroughly chilled.

Churn the custard in an ice-cream machine according to the manufacturer's instructions. Scoop the ice cream into a chilled 1.25 litre (42 fl oz/5 cup) container. Freeze for 1½–2 hours, to firm up before serving. If frozen for longer, leave it in the refrigerator for 20 minutes to soften slightly before serving.

To make the chocolate sauce, bring the cream to a boil in a saucepan over medium heat. Add the chocolate, cinnamon and a pinch of salt. Allow to stand for 1–2 minutes, then whisk until the chocolate has melted and the mixture is smooth. Serve warm, or cover and refrigerate for up to 2 days. Before serving, reheat the sauce using a double-boiler or microwave.

When ready to serve, combine the caster sugar, cinnamon and star anise in a large bowl.

For store-bought tortilla chips, preheat the oven to 170°C (340°F) fan-forced. Melt the 80 g (2¾ oz) butter and pour into a large bowl. Add the tortilla chips and toss until well coated in the butter. Working in batches, toss the chips in the spice sugar. Spread the spice-coated tortilla chips over a baking tray or baking dish suitable for serving. Bake for 4–5 minutes, or until the chips are warmed through and lightly toasted.

Top the store-bought tortilla chips with scoops of the ice cream, drizzle with the chocolate sauce and scatter with shredded orange zest. Serve immediately.

If using homemade tortilla chips, toss the hot chips in the spice sugar immediately after cooking them. There is no need to bake them, simply top with all the toppings and serve immediately.

DESSERT NACHOS WITH CINNAMON & ORANGE ICE CREAM

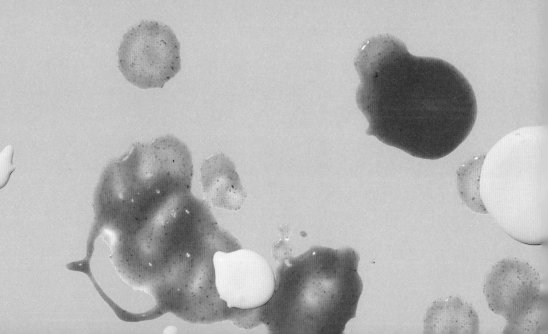

NOTCHOS

CRISPY LAMB SOUVLAKI & PITA NACHOS

SERVES 4

600 g (1 lb 5 oz) lamb forequarter chops, cut into strips, bones discarded

finely grated zest and juice of ½ lemon

1 garlic clove, crushed

1 teaspoon finely chopped fresh oregano

1 tablespoon olive oil

½ red onion, thinly sliced

2 tablespoons red wine vinegar

3 large pita breads, about 300 g (10½ oz)

olive oil spray, for cooking

dried oregano, for sprinkling

1 large tomato, cut into wedges

1 baby cos (romaine) lettuce, sliced lengthways into thin wedges

lemon wedges, to serve (optional)

GARLIC SAUCE

250 g (9 oz/1 cup) natural Greek-style yoghurt

1 garlic clove, crushed

2 teaspoons white wine vinegar

1 Lebanese (short) cucumber, grated, with the excess liquid squeezed out

Combine the lamb, lemon zest, lemon juice, garlic, fresh oregano and oil in a bowl. Toss to coat all the lamb, then cover and marinate in the refrigerator for 1 hour.

Meanwhile, combine the onion and vinegar in a separate bowl and set aside.

For the garlic sauce, whisk the yoghurt, garlic and vinegar together in a bowl until well combined. Stir in the grated cucumber. Stir in a little cold water to thin the consistency if necessary, then cover and refrigerate until required. Season to taste.

 Preheat the oven to 160°C (320°F) fan-forced. Spray the pita breads with olive oil, stack them on top of each other, then cut into wedges. Place them in a single layer over two baking trays, then sprinkle with dried oregano. Bake for 5 minutes, then turn and bake for a further 3–5 minutes, or until lightly browned and crisp. Remove from the oven and cool on the trays.

Meanwhile, heat a barbecue hotplate, chargrill pan or heavy-based frying pan over high heat. Working in batches if necessary, cook the lamb for 6–8 minutes, turning occasionally, until crispy around the edges and just cooked. (It's important not to over-crowd the cooking surface, to maintain a high heat.) Sprinkle generously with salt.

Pile the pita chips on a serving plate. Drizzle with about one-third of the garlic sauce. Top with the lamb, tomato, lettuce and pickled onion and drizzle with more garlic sauce. Serve immediately, with lemon wedges, and the remaining sauce on the side.

CRISPY LAMB
SOUVLAKI &
PITA NACHOS

POTATO CRISP & BACON NACHOS

SERVES 4

1 tablespoon vegetable oil

6 bacon rashers (slices), cut into thin strips

250 g (9 oz) plain crinkle-cut potato crisps

185 g (6½ oz/1½ cups) grated mature cheddar

150 g (5½ oz/1 cup) grated mozzarella

Guacamole (page 12), to serve (optional)

sour cream, to serve (optional)

1 spring onion (scallion), thinly sliced

Preheat the oven to 170°C (340°F) fan-forced.

Heat the oil in a frying pan over medium–high heat. Add the bacon and cook, stirring occasionally, for 5–6 minutes, or until crispy. Drain on paper towel.

Spread half the crisps over the base of a baking tray or baking dish suitable for serving. Combine the cheeses and scatter half over the crisps, followed by just less than half the bacon. Add layers of the remaining crisps, the remaining cheese and remaining bacon.

Bake for 5 minutes, or until the crisps are lightly toasted and the cheese is melted.

Top with the guacamole and sour cream, if using, or serve it on the side. Scatter with the spring onion and serve.

POTATO CRISP & BACON NACHOS

ITALIAN SAUSAGE RAGU & CIABATTA NACHOS

SERVES 4

2 tablespoons olive oil

6 pork and fennel sausages, about 600 g (1 lb 5 oz)

1 small onion, finely chopped

2 garlic cloves, crushed

1 celery stalk, finely chopped

1 small carrot, finely chopped

½ long red chilli, chopped

1 bay leaf

large handful of chopped parsley, including the stalks, plus extra leaves to serve

3 tablespoons tomato paste (concentrated purée)

80 ml (2½ fl oz/⅓ cup) white wine

400 g (14 oz) tin chopped tomatoes

240 g (8½ oz/2 cups) grated young asiago or mozzarella cheese

large handful of rocket (arugula)

shaved parmesan, to serve

CIABATTA CRISPS

1 garlic clove

350 g (12½ oz) loaf ciabatta bread, cut into 1 cm (½ inch) thick slices

2 tablespoons olive oil

Heat the oil in a large heavy-based frying pan over high heat. Remove the skins from the sausages and break up the sausage meat. Add to the pan and cook, stirring occasionally, for 6–8 minutes, or until browned. Transfer to a plate with a slotted spoon.

Reduce the heat and add the onion and garlic to the same pan. Cook, stirring, for 2–3 minutes, or until the garlic is fragrant. Add the celery, carrot, chilli, bay leaf and parsley and cook for 6–8 minutes, or until the vegetables are soft.

Add the tomato paste and cook, stirring, for 2 minutes, then deglaze the pan with the wine. Bring to the boil, add the chopped tomatoes, browned sausage meat and 125 ml (4 fl oz/½ cup) water and bring to the boil again. Season to taste with salt and freshly ground black pepper. Reduce the heat to low and simmer, stirring occasionally, for 15–20 minutes, or until the mixture is thickened and rich.

Meanwhile, for the ciabatta crisps, preheat the oven to 160°C (320°F) fan-forced. Cut the garlic clove in half horizontally and rub the cut sides of the garlic lightly over the bread slices. Brush the bread lightly all over with the oil and place in a single layer on several baking trays. Bake for 15–20 minutes, turning after 10 minutes, until lightly golden

and crisp. Remove from the oven and leave to cool while the ragu finishes cooking.

Increase the oven temperature to 170°C (340°F) fan-forced. Spread half the ciabatta crisps over the base of a baking tray or baking dish. Scatter with half the asiago or mozzarella and top with about half the ragu. Repeat with a second layer of ciabatta crisps, most of the cheese (reserve some for the top), the remaining ragu and then the remaining cheese.

Bake for 5 minutes, or until the cheese is melted. Top with the rocket, scatter with shaved parmesan and extra parsley, and serve immediately.

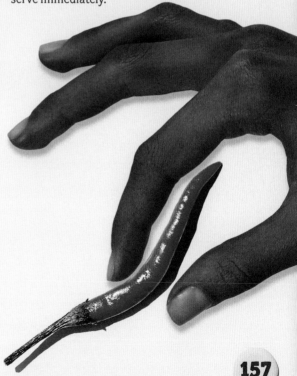

ITALIAN
SAUSAGE
RAGU &
CIABATTA
NACHOS

LOADED POTATO-SKIN NACHOS

SERVES 4

8 potatoes, about 1.2 kg (2 lb 10 oz), unpeeled and scrubbed

50 g (1¾ oz) butter, melted

1 tablespoon vegetable oil

4 bacon rashers (slices), cut into thin strips

1 onion, chopped

2 tablespoons tomato paste (concentrated purée)

2 garlic cloves, crushed

250 g (9 oz) minced (ground) pork

250 g (9 oz) minced (ground) veal

3 tablespoons sweet chilli sauce

2 teaspoons fish sauce or soy sauce

185 g (6½ oz/1½ cups) grated mature cheddar

1 quantity Tomato guacamole (page 12)

sour cream, to serve

pickled sliced jalapeño chillies, to serve

Preheat the oven to 180°C (350°F) fan-forced. Prick the potatoes all over with a knife and place them directly on the oven racks. Bake for 45–60 minutes, or until tender. Set aside until cool enough to handle, then cut the potatoes in half lengthways. Scoop out the flesh, leaving a 1 cm (½ inch) thick shell; reserve the flesh for another use. Cut each portion in half and place on a baking tray. Brush with the butter and bake for a further 20–25 minutes, or until crisp.

Meanwhile, heat the oil in a frying pan over medium–high heat. Add the bacon and cook, stirring occasionally, for 5–6 minutes, or until crispy. Transfer to a plate lined with paper towel, using a slotted spoon.

Reduce the heat to medium–low and cook the onion, stirring often, for 5–6 minutes, or until softened. Add the tomato paste and garlic and cook, stirring, for 2 minutes, or until fragrant.

Increase the heat to medium–high and add the pork and veal. Cook, stirring, for 6–8 minutes, or until the meat is well browned and starting to stick to the base of the pan. Stir in the chilli sauce and fish or soy sauce. Season with freshly ground black pepper to taste.

Pile the crisp potato skins over the base of a baking tray or baking dish suitable for serving. Top with the meat mixture and scatter with the cheese. Bake for 5 minutes, or until the cheese is melted.

Top with the guacamole and sour cream. Scatter with the bacon and chilli and serve immediately.

LOADED POTATO-SKIN NACHOS

SWEET POTATO NACHOS WITH MUSHROOM & LENTIL CHILLI

3 orange sweet potatoes, about 1.2 kg (2 lb 10 oz), unpeeled, scrubbed and sliced into 5 mm (¼ inch) rounds

1 tablespoon olive oil

1½ teaspoons smoked hot paprika

185 g (6½ oz/1½ cups) grated mature cheddar

1 quantity Roasted garlic guacamole (page 12)

sour cream, to serve

1 long red chilli, sliced

MUSHROOM & LENTIL CHILLI

1 tablespoon olive oil

1 onion, chopped

2 tablespoons tomato paste (concentrated purée)

2 teaspoons ground cumin

2 teaspoons chipotle chilli powder

2 garlic cloves, crushed

300 g (10½ oz) Swiss brown mushrooms, finely chopped

400 g (14 oz) tin chopped tomatoes

400 g (14 oz) tin brown lentils, drained

large handful of coriander (cilantro), including the stalks and leaves, chopped separately, plus extra to serve

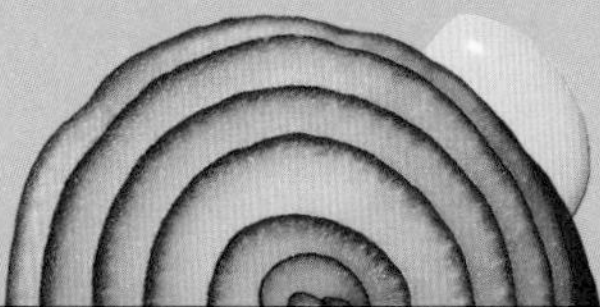

Preheat the oven to 180°C (350°F) fan-forced.

Toss the sweet potato slices with the oil until well coated. Spread in a single layer over several large baking trays. Sprinkle with the paprika and season to taste with salt and freshly ground black pepper. Bake for 30 minutes, or until tender, turning the slices over after 20 minutes.

Meanwhile, for the chilli, heat the oil in a large frying pan over medium–low heat and cook the onion, stirring occasionally, for 5–6 minutes, or until softened.

Add the tomato paste, cumin, chilli powder and garlic and cook, stirring, for 2 minutes. Increase the heat to medium–high and add the mushrooms and a good pinch of salt. Cook, stirring, for 6–8 minutes, or until softened.

Stir in the tomato, lentils, coriander stalks and 125 ml (4 fl oz/½ cup) water. Bring to the boil, then reduce the heat and simmer, uncovered, for about 4–5 minutes, or until slightly thickened. Stir in the coriander leaves and season to taste.

Pile the sweet potato over the base of four heatproof dishes or plates, or a large baking tray or baking dish suitable for serving.

Top with the chilli mixture and scatter with the cheese. Bake for 5 minutes, or until the cheese is melted.

Top with the guacamole and sour cream. Scatter with the chilli and serve immediately.

SWEET POTATO NACHOS WITH MUSHROOM & LENTIL CHILLI

THAI BEEF WONTON NACHOS

500 g (1 lb 2 oz) rump or sirloin steak

olive oil, for drizzling

vegetable oil, for deep-frying

200 g (7 oz) wonton wrappers, halved on the diagonal

250 g (9 oz) mixed cherry tomatoes, quartered

2 lemongrass stalks, pale section thinly sliced

10 kaffir lime leaves, finely shredded

large handful of mint leaves

kewpie mayonnaise, to serve

THAI DRESSING

3 Thai red chillies, chopped

2 garlic cloves

2 coriander (cilantro) roots, well washed and chopped

1 mint sprig, including the stem

3 tablespoons Thai fish sauce

3 tablespoons lime juice

1 teaspoon shaved palm sugar (jaggery)

For the dressing, use a mortar and pestle to pound the chilli, garlic, coriander, mint and a pinch of salt together until puréed. Stir in the Thai fish sauce, lime juice and palm sugar and mix well until the sugar has dissolved. Taste and add a little more fish sauce, lime juice or palm sugar to balance the flavour if necessary. Set aside.

Season the steak well with salt and freshly ground black pepper. Preheat a barbecue or chargrill pan on high. Drizzle the steak with a little olive oil and cook for 5–6 minutes for medium, turning occasionally, until a good crust forms and the steak is cooked to your liking. Transfer to a warm plate, spoon over about 2 tablespoons of the dressing, then cover lightly with foil and set aside to rest.

Pour some vegetable oil into a deep-fryer or large deep saucepan, to no more than one-third full. Heat the oil to 180°C (350°F) on a thermometer. In small batches, deep-fry the wrappers for 20–30 seconds, until just starting to change colour, turning them over after they have puffed up. Remove with a slotted spoon, drain on paper towel and season with salt.

Slice the beef thinly across the grain and place in a large bowl. Pour over the remaining dressing and mix well. Add the tomato, lemongrass and herbs and toss gently to combine.

Pile the wonton chips on a serving plate. Top with the beef, drizzle with mayonnaise and serve immediately.

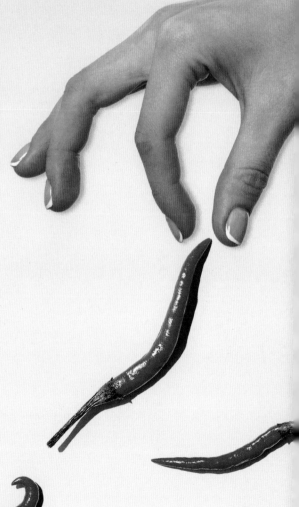

THAI BEEF WONTON NACHOS

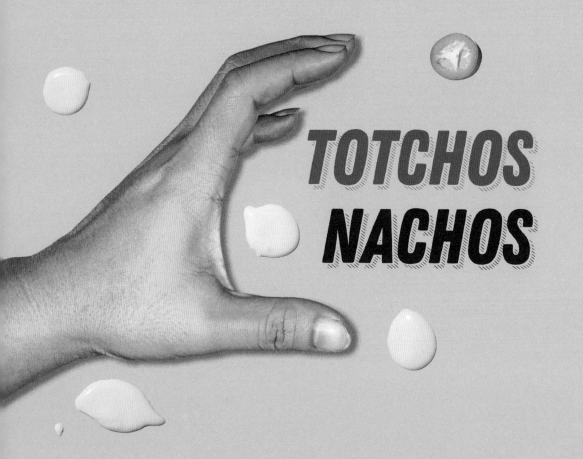

TOTCHOS NACHOS

SERVES 4

1 kg (2 lb 3 oz) packet of frozen tater tots (potato nuggets)

185 g (6½ oz/1½ cups) grated mature cheddar

1 quantity Chipotle guacamole (page 12)

1 quantity Refried beans (page 14), warmed

sliced pickled jalapeño chillies, to serve

queso fresco or feta, to serve

hot sauce, to serve

Preheat the oven to 210°C (410°F) fan-forced, with two baking trays in the oven. Spread the potato nuggets over the baking trays and bake for 10 minutes. Turn them over and bake for another 8–10 minutes, or until crisp. (Alternatively, prepare the potato nuggets following the packet directions.)

Reduce the oven temperature to 170°C (340°F) fan-forced. Spread half the cooked potato nuggets over the base of a baking tray or baking dish suitable for serving. Scatter with half the cheese, then top with the remaining potato nuggets and cheese.

Bake for 5 minutes, or until the cheese is melted. Top with the guacamole and refried beans. Scatter with chilli and cheese, drizzle with hot sauce and serve immediately.

**TOTCHOS
NACHOS**

WAFFLE NACHOS WITH CREAMY CORN CHEESE

SERVES 4

1 tablespoon vegetable oil

1 chorizo sausage, about 100 g (3½ oz), sliced

250 g (9 oz) packet of English-style waffles

1 quantity Pico de gallo (page 20)

chopped coriander (cilantro), to serve

CREAMY CORN CHEESE

250 g (9 oz/2 cups) grated mature cheddar

2 x 125 g (4½ oz) tins creamed corn

60 g (2 oz/¼ cup) good-quality mayonnaise

¼ small onion, finely chopped

SPICY BLACK BEANS

1 tablespoon olive oil

1 red onion, finely chopped

2 garlic cloves, crushed

400 g (14 oz) tin black beans, drained

1 tablespoon roughly chopped pickled jalapeño chilli

1 teaspoon ground cumin

handful of coriander (cilantro), chopped

Combine the creamy corn cheese ingredients in a bowl. Season to taste with salt and freshly ground black pepper.

For the beans, heat the oil in a frying pan over medium–low heat and cook the onion and garlic, stirring occasionally, for 6–8 minutes, or until tender. Add the beans, chilli, cumin and 80 ml (2½ fl oz/⅓ cup) water. Cook, stirring and mashing some of the beans, for 6–8 minutes, or until most of the liquid has evaporated. Stir in the coriander, then season to taste.

Preheat the oven to 170°C (340°F) fan-forced.

Heat the oil in a frying pan over medium–low heat. Cook the chorizo for 5–6 minutes, or until browned and a little crispy around the edges. Remove from the pan using a slotted spoon and drain on paper towel.

Meanwhile, heat the waffles according to the packet directions, then cut in half on the diagonal.

Spread half the waffles over the base of a baking tray or baking dish suitable for serving. Spoon a little less than half the beans and half the creamy corn cheese over the top. Repeat with a second layer of waffles, then the remaining beans and creamy corn cheese. Bake for 6–8 minutes, or until the cheese in the topping is melted.

Top with the chorizo and pico de gallo. Scatter with coriander and serve immediately.

WAFFLE NACHOS WITH CREAMY CORN CHEESE

BUÑUELOS WITH MAPLE BANANAS & PECANS

SERVES 4–6

SERVES 4–6

35 g (1½ oz/⅓ cup) pecans

165 g (6 oz/¾ cup) caster (superfine) sugar

2 teaspoons ground cinnamon

vegetable oil, for frying

30 g (1 oz) butter

60 ml (2 fl oz/¼ cup) maple syrup, plus extra to serve

3 firm ripe bananas, thickly sliced on the diagonal

coconut ice cream, to serve

edible flowers, to serve

BUÑUELOS

1 egg, beaten

80 ml (2½ fl oz/⅓ cup) full-cream (whole) milk

300 g (10½ oz/2 cups) plain (all-purpose) flour, plus extra for dusting

2 tablespoons caster (superfine) sugar

1 teaspoon baking powder

½ teaspoon salt

30 g (1 oz) butter, melted

To make the buñuelos, combine the egg and milk in a bowl. Sift the flour, sugar, baking powder and salt into a separate bowl, then stir into the egg mixture in two batches. Add the butter and mix until the dough comes together. (Alternatively, pulse the dry ingredients in a food processor until combined. Add the butter and pulse until the mixture is crumbly in appearance, then add the egg and process until the dough just comes together.)

Cover and set aside for 10 minutes. Turn out onto a lightly floured surface and knead for 2 minutes, or until smooth. Cover and set aside to rest for 20 minutes.

Meanwhile, in a heavy-based frying pan, cook the pecans for 4–5 minutes over medium heat, until toasted and fragrant. Transfer to a plate to a cool, then roughly chop and set aside.

Divide the dough into 32 even portions. On a very lightly floured surface, roll them out into circles about 10 cm (4 inches) in diameter. Brush off any excess flour.

Combine the caster sugar and cinnamon in a large bowl.

Add enough oil to a heavy frying pan for shallow frying; you'll need a depth of about 3 cm (1¼ inches). Heat the oil to 180°C

(350°F) on a thermometer. Cook the pastries, a few at a time, for 30–60 seconds on each side, or until browned all over. Drain on paper towel and dust immediately with the cinnamon sugar.

Meanwhile, melt the butter in the same frying pan you used for the pecans. Add the maple syrup and banana slices and cook for 5–6 minutes, or until caramelised, turning carefully after 3–4 minutes.

Pile the warm buñuelos on a serving plate, then top with the bananas and any sauce from the pan. Add scoops of ice cream, scatter with the pecans and edible flowers, and drizzle with extra maple syrup. Serve immediately.

NOTE

If the buñuelos are puffing up too much when cooked, prick the dough a few times with a fork before serving.

BUÑUELOS WITH MAPLE BANANAS & PECANS

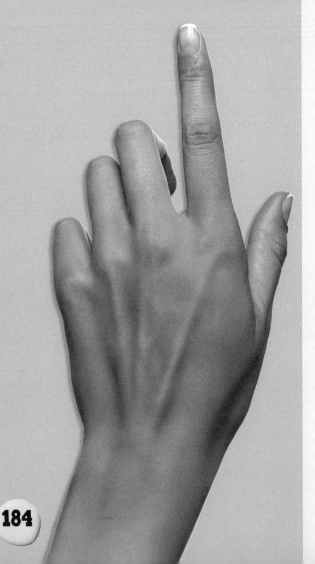

S'MORES NACHOS

SERVES 6–8

240 g (8½ oz/2⅔ cups) marshmallows, excess powdery coating brushed off, roughly chopped

150 g (5½ oz) dark chocolate, roughly chopped

40 g (1½ oz/¼ cup) roasted salted peanuts, roughly chopped

GRAHAM CRACKERS
(MAKES ABOUT 60)

225 g (8 oz/1½ cups) plain (all-purpose) flour

150 g (5½ oz/1 cup) wholemeal (whole-wheat) flour, plus extra for dusting

165 g (6 oz/¾ cup, firmly packed) muscavado sugar

1 teaspoon baking powder

1 teaspoon ground cinnamon

½ teaspoon salt

125 g (4½ oz) cold unsalted butter, chopped

175 g (6 oz/½ cup) golden syrup or honey

1 tablespoon vanilla bean paste

To make the crackers, combine the flours, sugar, baking powder, cinnamon and salt in a food processor and pulse until combined. Add the butter and pulse until the mixture is grainy in appearance. Add the remaining ingredients and pulse until the dough comes together.

Scoop the dough onto a piece of plastic wrap. Pat into a flat square shape, about 3 cm (1¼ inches) thick, and refrigerate for 2 hours, or for as long as overnight, until firm.

Preheat the oven to 160°C (320°F) fan-forced. Line two large baking trays with baking paper.

Cut the dough in half. Place the dough between two sheets of non-stick baking paper, or dust your work surface lightly with flour. Roll the dough out into a rectangle about 3 mm (⅛ inch) thick. Cut the dough into strips about 6 cm (2½ inches) wide, then cut each strip into triangles. Vary the size of the triangles if you like. Transfer the triangles to a baking tray, then prick each one several times with a fork, or the blunt end of a bamboo skewer.

Repeat with the other piece of dough, re-rolling the scraps as necessary. Refrigerate the dough if it becomes too soft to handle.

Bake for 13–15 minutes, or until the crackers are lightly browned and just starting to colour underneath. Transfer to a wire rack to cool.

Pile half the crackers on a heatproof serving plate or baking tray suitable for serving. Top with about half the marshmallows and half the chocolate, then the remaining crackers, chocolate and marshmallows.

Bake at 160°C (320°F) fan-forced for 4–5 minutes, or until the chocolate has melted and the marshmallows start to brown. Scatter with the peanuts and serve immediately.

NOTES

Use a kitchen blow torch or place the nachos under a hot grill (broiler) for a few minutes if you need a bit of extra browning at the end, being careful not to burn the chocolate.

This recipe is also good made with store-bought digestive biscuits.

S'MORES
NACHOS

INDEX

R

Refried beans 14

Roast veg nachos with feta dressing 106

Roast vegetables 106

Roasted capsicum & tomato salsa 16

Roasted garlic guacamole 12

Roasted onion & tomato salsa 16

Roasted tomato salsa 16

S

S'mores nachos 184

Salmon ceviche nachos 130

Sauces & Salsas

    4-cheese beer sauce 95

    Baja sauce 29

    Blue cheese sauce 86

    Charred pepper salsa 57

    Cheese sauce 32

    Chimichurri sauce 53

    Chipotle guacamole 12

    Chipotle hollandaise 75

    Chipotle mayo 18

    Coriander & mint pesto 68

    Crema 131

    Feta dressing 106

    Garlic aïoli 18

    Garlic sauce 148

    Grilled corn salsa 134

    Guacamole 12

    Mango & jicama salsa 68

    Mexican chocolate sauce 142

    Mustard aïoli 91

Pico de gallo 20

Roasted capsicum & tomato salsa 16

Roasted garlic guacamole 12

Roasted onion & tomato salsa 16

Roasted tomato salsa 16

Smoky BBQ sauce 60

Thai dressing 168

Tomatillo guacamole 12

Tomato guacamole 12

Sausage nachos with 4-cheese beer sauce 94

sausage ragu & ciabatta nachos, Italian 156

Smoky BBQ sauce 60

souvlaki & pita nachos, Crispy lamb 148

Spicy black beans 177

steak nachos, Chimichurri 52

Street corn nachos 64

Sweet

    Buñuelos with maple bananas & pecans 180

    Caramelised apple dessert nachos 138

    S'mores nachos 184

Sweet potato nachos with mushroom & lentil chilli 164

T

Texas-style chicken nachos with mango & jicama salsa 68

Thai beef wonton nachos 168

Thai dressing 168

tinga, Chicken 48

Tomatillo guacamole 12

Tomato guacamole 12

tomato nachos with corn salsa, Lentil & roasted 134

tomato salsa, Roasted 16

tomato salsa, Roasted capsicum & 16

tomato salsa, Roasted onion & 16

Top-shelf nachos 122

Totchos nachos 172

V

Vegan loaded nachos 126

Vegetarian

    Bruschetta nachos with kale crisps 82

    Cheeseboard nachos 78

    Chilaquiles 36

    Lentil & roasted tomato nachos with corn salsa 134

    Roast veg nachos with feta dressing 106

    Street corn nachos 64

    Sweet potato nachos with mushroom & lentil chilli 164

    Totchos nachos 172

    Vegan loaded nachos 126

W

Waffle nachos with creamy corn cheese 176

wonton nachos, Thai beef 168

Published in 2018 by Smith Street Books
Collingwood | Melbourne | Australia
smithstreetbooks.com

ISBN: 978-1-925418-74-3

Copyright recipes, text & design © Smith Street Books
Recipe and ingredient photography © Chris Middleton
Stock photography © Adobe Stock

CIP data is available from the National Library of Australia

Publisher: Paul McNally
Editor: Katri Hilden
Recipe development: Caroline Griffiths
Design concept: Stephanie Spartels
Design layout: Heather Menzies, Studio31 Graphics
Photographer: Chris Middleton
Art director & Stylist: Stephanie Stamatis
Food preparation: Caroline Griffiths & Emma Roocke

Printed & bound in China by C&C Offset Printing Co., Ltd.

Book 58
10 9 8 7 6 5 4 3 2 1